(and Other Spinning Toys)

by Beth Dvergsten Stevens

Book Design: Jan M. Michalson
Cover Illustration: Michael Aspengren
Inside Illustration: Michael Aspengren

Dedication

For all children who love the magic and challenge of spin toys. With special thanks to my son and his buddies for their expert yo-yo help.

About the Author

Beth Stevens is a writer and former teacher. She currently writes stories and develops crafts and games for children's magazines. She also writes a weekly newspaper column for kids. Her first book, *Celebrate Christmas Around the World,* was a teacher's resource book.

Although she's no longer in the classroom, she still loves teaching and learning. She hopes her readers will discover something new and interesting every time they open one of her books! Beth lives in Waverly, Iowa, with her husband, three children, and their pets.

Image credits: Mindy Lage pp. 3, 6–8, 10, 11, 19–28, 37; Mike Aspengren p. 18
Lucky Meisenheimer (from *Lucky's Collectors' Guide to 20th Century Yo-Yos.*) p. 17
Tops courtesy Don Olney (www.toycrafter.com) pp. 8 (middle), 22 (top), 25

Contents

Perfection Learning®

History of Tops

Around and around they go. Where will they stop? Nobody knows. Maybe they'll spin forever!

Tops have been spinning for thousands of years. People in every part of the world had tops.

But not all tops were toys. Some tops were weapons.

Ancient island people hunted with sling stones. Sling stones looked like peg tops. Do you think hunters played with them after hunting?

Some tops made music. Ancient Maori people had tops that hummed. They sang

ancient—very, very old

songs with them. This music made the fighters feel better after battle.

Some tops were gifts. Ancient people gave them to their gods. They were **ceramic** or clay. And they were beautiful.

Even in ancient times, some people played games with tops. Sometimes the dead were

ceramic—a clay that has been baked at very high temperatures

buried with tops. Then they would have something to play with in the afterlife.

What were the first toy tops like? They were very simple. They were made from common things like pinecones or potatoes.

They were thorns stuck through berries. Some were pointed rocks. Children practiced until they could spin their tops well.

Make your own simple top. Find a hard crabapple or cherry. Poke a toothpick through it. Then set it on the floor. And twirl it between your fingers. It won't spin very long. But it's fun to watch!

Many people think the first tops were made in Japan or China. But children in Greece, Egypt, and Rome played with tops. So did children in Persia and India. Ancient tops have even been found in Bolivia and on South Pacific islands.

Tops were probably invented in different places. By different people. At different times. Why? All people liked to watch things spin. And all people liked to have fun!

China and Japan had many kinds of tops. There were fighting tops, catching tops, whistling tops, and humming tops.

Some tops had tiny lanterns. And some were whipping tops to spin on ice or dirt.

Some tops were carved from wood. Others were cut from stone or **ivory**. Some tops were formed from clay or bone. Others were made from shells or metal.

ivory—creamy white material found in elephant, walrus, and whale tusks

Most early tops were twirlers, peg tops, or whip tops. Some even hummed.

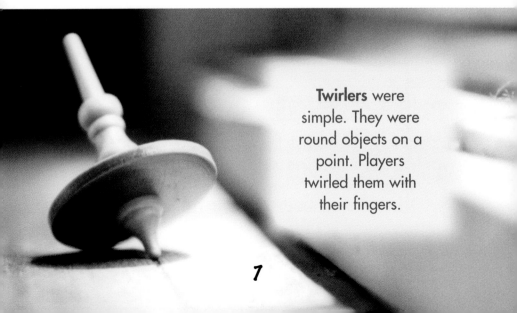

Twirlers were simple. They were round objects on a point. Players twirled them with their fingers.

Peg tops had tall stems. Players wrapped a cord around the stem. They threw peg tops to the ground. Then they pulled the cord off. These tops spun fast. Peg tops were often carved from wood. The peg end was pointed. Sometimes the tip was bone or metal. It was hard. Then it wouldn't break when it hit the ground.

Whip tops were big. They could spin for a long time. Why? Players stroked them over and over with a long whip.

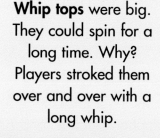

Humming tops made noise. They were hollow. And they had holes in the sides. When they spun, air went into the holes. They hummed or whistled!

As people traveled to other lands, they saw many tops. They liked them. So they traded for tops.

These traders brought the tops home to their children. Soon tops and other spin toys were everywhere.

People from Asia brought tops to North America. They traveled across the Bering Strait.

They traded their tops for Eskimo things. Eskimo children became good top spinners.

Other tops came to America on ships. People from France and England brought them. Soon tops became a favorite toy in America.

Tops were very popular during the Depression. Why? Families didn't have much money. And tops were cheap and fun!

Some of today's tops are metal or wood. But most of them are plastic.

They come in all sizes. They are colorful.

Some have blinking lights. Others have music or whistles. Some have springs or spiral pumps. And others have special pieces to launch them.

Yes, there are many kinds of tops. But all tops spin on an **axis** or **axle**. They're like magic!

People like to watch them. That's why they are still popular today.

axis—a straight line or pin that has an object spinning around it
axle—a pin that has a wheel spinning on it

CHAPTER 2

History of Yo-Yos and Other Spin Toys

People like tops. But there are other spin toys too. Look at these.

Yo-Yos

A yo-yo is a top on a string. It spins down and up just like magic.

It seems new to us. But the yo-yo was invented long ago. It was used as a weapon in early times.

In the Philippines, fighters threw stone yo-yos at their enemies. If they missed, they pulled on the string. Then they grabbed the stone and threw it again.

But yo-yos were used for fun too. The early Greeks played with them. So did people in Japan and China.

In the Philippines, fathers carved yo-yos for their children. Many Filipinos were expert yo-yo spinners!

What does the word *yo-yo* mean? Where does it come from? Yo-yo means "come-come" or "to return." It comes from the Philippines.

People in Europe didn't know about yo-yos until the 1790s. **Missionaries** brought them back to France. The French people thought yo-yos were great.

missionary—a person who travels and teaches religion to others

Soon there were many yo-yos in France. Who played with them? Children didn't. Rich adults did. Even kings played with them!

But then something happened. There was a **revolution** in France. Many rich people had to leave. They went to other countries in Europe. They took their yo-yos with them.

revolution—a war between the government and the people of a country

By the 1800s, yo-yos were all over Europe. Then Europeans brought their yo-yos to America.

In 1866, factories started making yo-yos. Americans bought them. They were easy to use.

A string was tied to the axle. But these yo-yos just rolled down and up. They couldn't do tricks.

In 1928, the yo-yo changed. All because Donald Duncan met Pedro Flores.

Flores was from the Philippines. He had played with yo-yos since he was little. And he owned a yo-yo factory.

Crowds of people watched Flores do yo-yo tricks. He made his yo-yos **sleep** at the end of the string. The crowds cheered!

> **sleep**—keep spinning at the end of the string

That looks like fun! Duncan thought. I think children would like these toys.

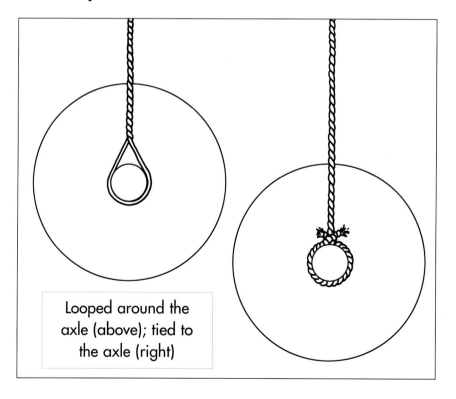

Looped around the axle (above); tied to the axle (right)

Duncan found out how Flores made his yo-yos. His string wasn't tied to the axle. It was just looped on. These yo-yos could "sleep" and do tricks.

So Duncan bought Pedro Flores' factory. He made lots of wooden yo-yos.

Then he hired yo-yo experts to give shows everywhere. His company grew. Duncan yo-yos became famous.

Yo-yos were very popular for a while. Especially in the 1920s and 1930s.

Then people quit playing with them. The yo-yo **fad** died out.

In the 1960s, people started playing with yo-yos again. They learned new tricks. They held contests. And they won prizes.

fad—something that's popular for a short time. Everyone loves it. Then people lose interest. Later, it becomes popular again with different people. Fads come and go.

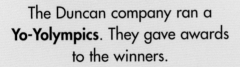

The Duncan company ran a **Yo-Yolympics**. They gave awards to the winners.

Factories sold 16 million yo-yos a year! Some were wood. But most were plastic. They were bright, colorful, and cheap.

Some yo-yos sparked or made music. Some were shaped like footballs or golf balls. Some glowed in the dark. Some even lit up.

You can still buy Duncan yo-yos today. There are other brands too.

Some new yo-yos have clutches and ball bearings. It's easier to do tricks with these.

But all yo-yos fit into your pocket. And it's fun take them wherever you go!

Other Spin Toys

There are other old spin toys too. One is the **diabolo**. It is also called a *diablo* or *devil on two sticks*.

A diabolo looks like an hourglass. It is played on a string hooked to two sticks. The diabolo spins along the string. A good player can throw the diabolo up and catch it on the string! If it spins fast, it hums.

People in China played with diabolos for hundreds of years. Travelers brought them to France and England.

Jugglers entertained kings with their diabolos. Napoleon, a French ruler, was very good at this game.

Diabolos came to the United States from Mexico and England. And some American Indian tribes played with them. But they weren't popular in the United States until the 1900s.

Buzzers or **whirligigs** have been around for centuries too. Children everywhere had these tops. They were easy to make and fun to spin. They buzzed.

Buzzers were made of many things. Eskimos used a leather disk on a cord. American Indians used a piece of bone, gourd, or pottery. The people in New Guinea used a shell. In Europe and America, children used a flat button.

The **thaumatrope** was invented in 1825. It is a flat cardboard circle on strings. It has a different picture on each side. When it spins fast, both pictures go together. The player sees just one. This toy led to the invention of movies.

Every spin toy is different. But each type is fun to spin.

CHAPTER 3

Name That Top!

Twirler

This is the simplest top. Players spin it with their hands.

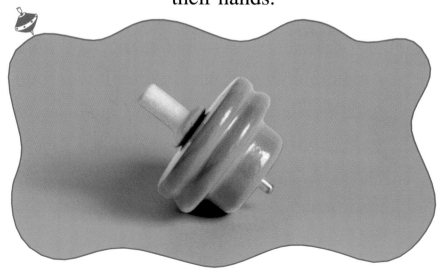

21

- The first twirler was a thorn stuck through a berry or seed.
- Teetotums and dreidels are twirlers.

Teetotem—a game top with four sides. Gamblers used teetotums. They spun the top. Sometimes it landed on a lucky side. They lost money if it didn't! Some teetotems were like dice. They had six sides with numbers.

The **dreidel** is a four-sided teetotum used in Hanukkah games. It has Hebrew letters on each side.

Supported Top

A cord is wrapped around its tall stem.
It spins longer than a twirler.

- Players hold the top on the ground while the cord is pulled off.
- A special tool holds some tops in place. It fits over the stem. The tool is taken off when the top begins to spin.

Peg Top

This top is wrapped with a cord
and thrown to the ground.

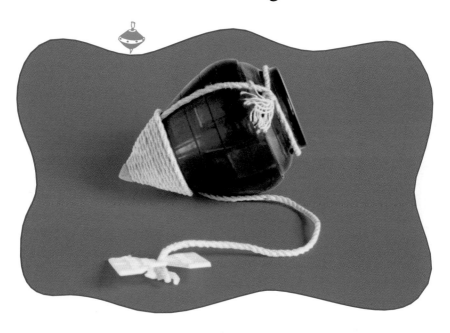

- Sometimes a groove holds the cord.
- It takes lots of practice to throw a peg top well!
- Peg tops were used in contests. They were spun on dirt.
- Swivel tops are a type of peg top. They have a loop for the cord. Swivel tops are dropped, not thrown.

Whip Top

A leather whip helped this top
spin for a long time.

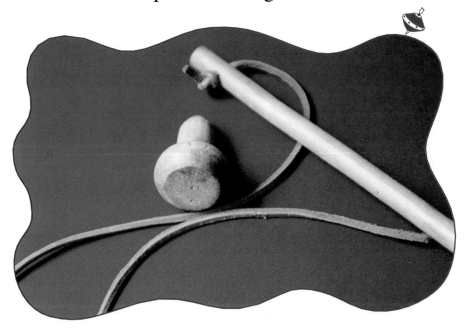

- These tops kept spinning as long as players whipped them.
- Whip tops were popular long ago. Children don't play with these anymore.
- They were shaped like pinecones. Some were heavy.
- They were used on smooth, hard surfaces. Even ice!

Buzzer (Whizzer, Whirligig, Magic Wheel, Rhombus)

This flat top spins on a string
and makes noise.

- A player winds up the top and string. It hums or buzzes when it spins.
- It spins one way when you pull your hands out. It spins the other way when you move your hands together.
- Tops with holes or jagged edges make more noise.

Yo-Yo

This top moves down and up on a string.

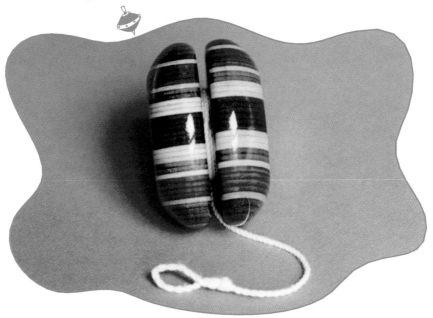

- A string is wrapped around the center axle.
- The string's other end is around the player's middle finger.
- A player throws the yo-yo toward the ground. It spins down the string. Then it spins back up. The player catches it in her hand.
- Throwing a yo-yo hard and fast makes it spin longer.
- The best yo-yos for beginners are Butterfly and Imperial.

Other Spinning Toys

Gyroscope

Flight Ring

Wheelo

Frisbee

Sky Top

Make Your Own Spin Toys!

Children carved tops from wood. They cut yo-yos and diabolos from spools or dried gourds. They made buzzers from bones or buttons. They used pencils and sticks for axles and axes.

You can make your own spin toys too! Just follow these directions.

Twirl Tops

Needs

a round flat metal juice lid or a
    flat canning lid
thick cardboard
3 Styrofoam® plates
roofing nail, pencil, or small dowel for axis
rubber bands
old thread spool
hammer
markers
stickers
pencil sharpener

Steps for a metal top

1. Ask an adult for help. Pound a roofing nail through the center of the metal lid.

2. The point of the nail should stick out ¾". Wrap a rubber band around the nail above and below the lid.

Steps for a cardboard top

1. Cut a 3½" circle from the cardboard. Use a compass or trace around a plastic lid.
2. Decorate one side.
3. Ask an adult to help cut a 4" piece of dowel. Sharpen one end. Or use a short pencil. Push point through center of circle.

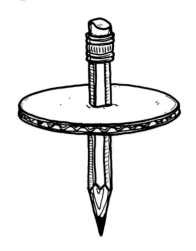

Steps for a plate top

1. Use a 7" sharpened pencil or dowel.
2. Push the pointed end through the bottom of three plates at the center. Point should stick out about 3".
3. Slide a spool onto the point. Push it against the plate.
4. Wrap a rubber band around pencil or dowel point and push it up against the spool.
5. Wrap another rubber band around the top of the pencil or dowel. Push it down against the plate.

Thaumatropes and Buzzers

Needs

heavy poster board

string

scissors

ruler

permanent markers

paper punch

pencil

Steps for a thaumatrope

1. Draw a 3½" circle on the cardboard. Cut it out carefully.
2. Punch a hole on two opposite edges of the circle as shown.
3. Cut two pieces of string that are 12" long.
4. Tie a string through each hole and knot ends.
5. Choose two things that go together, such as

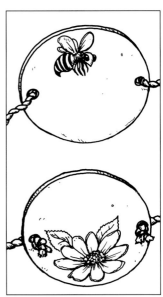

flowers in a vase, a person in jail, a bird in a tree, or the stars in the sky.

6. Place holes at the sides and draw <u>one</u> picture on the circle.

7. Turn the circle over with the bottom edge up. Draw the second picture.

8. Spin it and watch the pictures go together. (See spinning directions in Chapter 5.)

Steps for a buzzer

1. Draw a 3½" circle on the cardboard. Cut it out carefully.

2. Use the point of a pencil or scissors to make two holes near the center of the circle. It looks like a big button. Ask an adult to help with this.

3. Cut a piece of string that is 50" to 60" long.

4. Put the string through the holes. Tie the string ends together.

5. Decorate the circle with markers.

6. Spin it and listen. (See spinning directions in Chapter 5.)

Variations

- Punch holes or cut Vs around outside edges to make it buzz louder.

- If your cardboard is too light, glue two circles together.

- Want to make a quick button buzzer? Find a big flat button. Put the long string through the holes and tie it. It's ready to spin!

Cardboard Yo-Yo

Needs

clean cardboard from a pizza box

1-pound coffee can

scissors

glue

3" pencil

string

small rubber bands

empty thread spool (optional)

Steps

1. Draw around a 1-pound coffee can on the cardboard. Do this six times. Cut out the circles carefully.

2. Glue three circles together to make one disk. Only glue around the outer edges. Try not to glue the center. Do the same with the other three circles.

3. Set the disks under a heavy book for five minutes.

4. Mark the centers of the disks. Set them on top of a large piece of cardboard. Push a pencil tip through the center of each disk to create holes.

5. Push the pencil tip through the hole in one disk. Move the disk toward the eraser end.

6. Cut a piece of string about 45" long. Tie one end around the pencil.

7. Push the pencil tip through the hole in the other disk. The disks should be about ½" apart. Center them on the pencil. The string will be between.

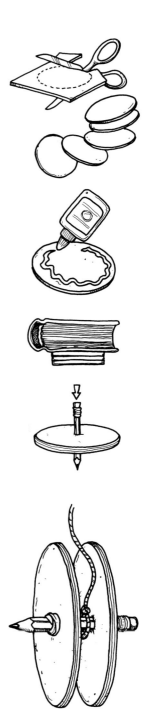

8. Wind rubber bands around the pencil ends to hold disks in place.
9. Wind up the string and try out your yo-yo.

Options

- For a faster spin—Put a spool axle between the cardboard disks. Tie the string to the spool.

- For a big, easy yo-yo—Use eight small paper plates instead of the six cardboard circles. Don't glue them together. Use a pencil or spool axle. Then follow the steps above.

CHAPTER 5

Amaze Your Friends!

Basic Skills, Games, and Tricks

It takes a lot of practice to make tops spin well. But it's worth it! Learn the basics first. Then try some tricks.

Top Talent
How to Spin Tops

Twirler Top

1. Set the top on the floor.

2. Grasp the stem between your thumb and first two fingers.
3. Turn your fingers and thumb in the opposite directions and let go.

Variations

- Hold the top just above the floor. Spin the stem and drop it.
- Turn it between your palms if the stem is long enough.

Supported Top

1. Wrap a cord around the stem.
2. Hold the point on the floor.
3. Pull the cord and let go of the top.
4. If you have a tool, lift it off when the top spins.

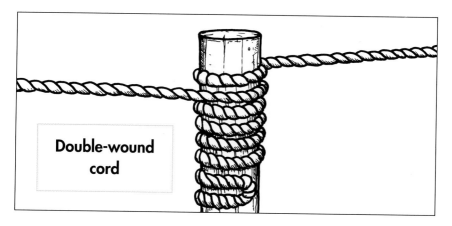

Double-wound cord

Peg Top

Always play with this top outside.

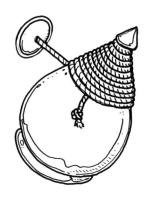

1. Wrap the cord tightly around top end.

2. Put button end of cord between two fingers on top of your hand.

3. Hold top in your hand with thumb on peg.

4. Kneel down. Hold top about a foot above the ground.

5. Pull your arm back and toss the top forward at the ground.

6. Let go of the top and yank back on the cord. It should land and spin.

How to wrap a peg top
Bring the cord down toward peg. Wrap the cord around the top, starting near peg. Work up. Keep wrapping the cord tightly. Don't overlap wrappings.

Twirler, Supported, and Peg Top Games

Longest Spin Games

- Use a stop watch. See how long your top will spin.

- Each player has three to five twirler tops. Someone says "Go." The players start their tops. The winner is the first player to get all five tops spinning at the same time. Players can restart tops that stop.

Target Games

- Draw a circle in dirt. Toss your peg top toward the target. Make it land and spin inside the circle.

- Place pennies inside a circle. Throw your peg top toward them. Try to knock them out of the circle with your top.

- Draw a chalk circle. Divide it into 10 different-sized spaces. Mark each space 1 to 10. The smallest piece is 10. Spin your tops and see where they land. Add up your points.

- Two players spin their tops at the same time. Players try to knock each other's top over. But the winning top has to keep spinning!

> Expert peg top spinners can
> - spin a top on their nose or open hand
> - make the top come back to them before it hits the ground
> - use the string to pick up a spinning peg top

Go Bonkers for Buzzers
How to Spin a Buzzer

1. Put your thumbs into the string loops. Slide the buzzer to the middle.
2. Let the string and buzzer hang down. Flip the buzzer around many times until string is twisted tightly. String will feel snug around thumbs.
3. Pull out on both strings. The buzzer will spin fast. When string is almost untwisted, move your hands closer together. Let

buzzer and string rewind in the other direction. Then pull out on strings again.

4. Keep moving hands together and apart so buzzer keeps spinning. Then listen. Do you hear the buzzing?

Buzzer Tricks

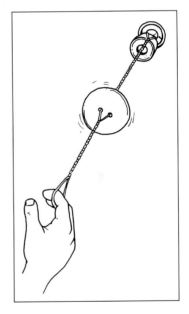

- Put one loop around a doorknob. Hold the other loop like usual. Pull and loosen string with one hand.
- Wind up the buzzer. Sit down and put loops around your big toes. Spin the buzzer with your feet!
- Spin your buzzer. Then set its edge on the floor with the strings loose. Watch the buzzer roll forward.

Yo-Yo Know-How
How To Spin A Yo-Yo

Get Ready!

1. Hold the yo-yo on the floor between your feet.
2. Pull the string up. The end should reach your waist.
3. Tie a small loop at the end of the string. Then pull some more string through this loop for a slip knot.
4. Hold the yo-yo in your left hand. Wind the string around the axle with your right hand.*
5. Put your middle finger into the slip knot.

Winding the String
If the string doesn't catch right away, wind it over your finger first. Then take your finger out and pull the string tight.

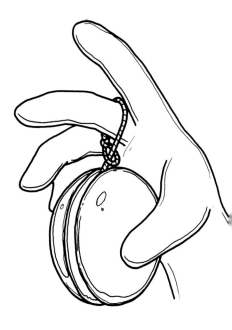

*For Lefties: Hold the yo-yo in your right hand. Wind the string with your left hand.

44

Get Set with Gravity Pulls!

For beginners—Hold the yo-yo with hand on top. Jerk your wrist down and let go of the yo-yo. When it gets to the end of the string, pull your hand up. The yo-yo will roll back up.

For a faster spin—Throw it harder. Hold the yo-yo in your hand, palm up. Bend your elbow. Bring yo-yo toward your shoulder. Throw your wrist and yo-yo forward and down. When the yo-yo gets to the end of the string, turn your hand over. Jerk your hand up and the yo-yo will climb back up the string.

Changing the String on a Yo-Yo

Don't buy a new yo-yo if the string is worn out. Just put on a new string.

To remove an old string—Don't cut it. Just untwist string at axle. Spread loop open and take the yo-yo off.

To put on a new string—Untwist new string at folded end. Hold it open and put the loop around axle. Twist it again.

Go with Yo-Yo Tricks

It's easy to do tricks with a "dead" yo-yo. That's one that is not spinning! But can you do them while it's "alive" and spinning? Will it come back to you?

- **Sleeper**—Throw the yo-yo down. But don't pull it back up right away. Instead, let it spin, or sleep, at the end of the string for a few seconds. But before it stops spinning, pull it up to your hand. With practice, you'll know how long to let it sleep.

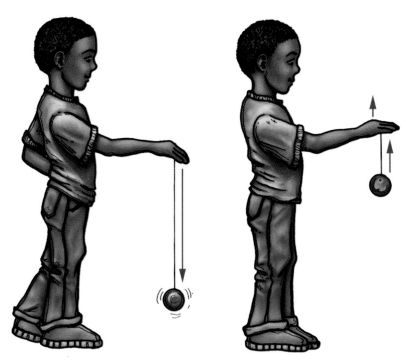

How long can a yo-yo sleep?
Start counting from the time the yo-yo leaves your hand.
2 to 4 seconds—Good for beginners
5 to 9 seconds—For those with more practice
10 or more seconds—Terrific!

- **Walk the Dog**—Put your yo-yo into a sleeper. Then set it lightly on the floor and let it roll forward. It looks like you're taking the dog for a walk! Pull it back to your hand before it stops spinning.

- **Forward Pass**—You might want to try this outside. Hold the yo-yo down at your side. The palm faces back. Swing your arm back, then forward. Flip your wrist up and throw the yo-yo out in front of you. Quickly turn your hand palm up. Pull on the string so the yo-yo comes back to your hand.

- **Around the World**—Go outside for this trick. Hold the yo-yo down at your side. The palm faces back. Swing your arm and throw it like a forward pass. Let it sleep and then swing it around in a big circle. Pull on the string so it comes back to your hand.

Learn these tricks and amaze your friends.
- Rock the Baby
- Eiffel Tower
- Sleeping Beauty
- Loop the Loop
- Skin the Cat
- Double Waterfall into the Pocket

Yo-Yo Hints

- Don't use a string that's too long. Your yo-yo could hit the ground and break.
- Throw one "gravity pull" before every trick. This smooths the string.
- If the string gets too twisted, let the yo-yo hang down and spin around. When it stops spinning, wind it up again.
- If the string gets too dirty or worn, put on a new one. Check the whole string for frays.

Thaumatrope Thrills
How to Spin a Thaumatrope

1. Put your thumbs through the strings.
2. Turn the circle many times until the string is twisted tightly.
3. Pull out on the strings and watch. As the circle spins, the two pictures turn into one.

Thaumatrope Game

- Surprising Shows—Draw one object on a disk. Ask a friend to draw an object on another disk. Then trade disks. Look at your friend's drawing. Draw a funny object on the other side of the disks. Trade again and spin your thaumatropes.

Top Trivia

Early Tops

- One 3000-year-old top was made of turquoise.
- Some old tops were made from wooden spinning wheels.
- Almost all American Indian tribes had whip tops. Ojibways made their tops from acorns. Dakota tops were made from animal horns. Nootka Indians made humming tops from bone or ivory. Maricopa Indians made tops from baked clay.
- Some boys used horse manure to hold the pegs in their peg tops! It acted like cement.

Early Top Games

- In the Appalachian Mountains, children whittled wooden spools to sharp points. They put pegs in the holes.

  Then they collected tin tags from chewing tobacco. They put the tags in a circle. They tried to knock the tags out of the circle with their tops. Try this with pennies today.

- Eskimo children spun their twirlers inside. Then they ran out and around the house. They tried to get back inside before their tops stopped spinning.

- Players had to decide who would go first in contests. So one boy spit on the dirt. Then players tossed their tops at the wet spot. The player who got closest, won.

- People used eel skin to make whips for whip tops. It was very soft. Whips were also made from animal tendons, hides, or woven cording.

Famous Spinners

- Billy the Kid was a Western outlaw. He was also a good diabolo spinner. He carried a diabolo in his saddlebags. He showed off in saloons.
- Tommy Smothers was called The Yo-Yo-Man. He liked to do yo-yo tricks. He did them every week on *The Smothers Brothers Comedy Hour* television program.
- In 1985, the NASA astronauts tried yo-yo tricks during a shuttle flight into space!

In Other Words . . .

Other names for tops
Dutch—*tol*
Portuguese—*piao*
French—*toupie*
Italian—*trottola*
Spanish—*peonza*
Latin—*turbo*

Other names for yo-yos
Dutch—*driftol*
Greek—*disc*
Old English—*bandalor* or *quiz*
French—*L 'Émigrette* or *joujou*

Other names for a buzzer
whirligig
whizzer
magic wheel
rhombus

Amazing Facts

- Some of the first yo-yos were carved from the horns of water buffalo.
- Every hour, 6,500 Duncan yo-yos are made!
- The world's biggest yo-yo was 256 pounds and 50" tall. The string was a thick rope. It was spun from a tall crane.
- A 15" yo-yo weighing 4 pounds was spun from a window. That window was on the tenth floor of a tall building!
- Dale Oliver, a yo-yo expert, made his yo-yo go "Around the World" 27 times in a row!
- One top in Malaysia spun for 100 minutes on a smooth metal surface.
- Many professionals use a new string **every** time they use a yo-yo.

Science and Spinning Facts

- The best spinners are balanced.
- Heavy tops spin longer than light ones.
- Wide tops spin longer than narrow ones.
- Narrow tops spin faster than wide tops.
- Tops with long pegs won't spin too long.
- A spinning top will stand up on its point. A top that is **not** spinning can't stand alone.
- A top starts to wobble before it falls over.